THE COLD HEART
WITH A STRONG MIND TO SURVIVE:

THE COLD HEART
WITH A STRONG MIND TO SURVIVE:

No Emotions, No Mercy, No Chance

VALERIA SAMUEL

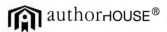

AuthorHouse™ LLC
1663 Liberty Drive
Bloomington, IN 47403
www.authorhouse.com
Phone: 1-800-839-8640

Published by AuthorHouse   2/14/2014

ISBN: 978-1-4918-6582-8 (sc)
ISBN: 978-1-4918-6581-1 (e)

Library of Congress Control Number: 2014903155

Autobiographical Description

Please look forward to the "Cold Heart with a Strong Mind," in the near future to become a fantastic play or movie.

Valeria's terrifying true events are appealing, break necking, and filled with interesting events that will keep you at the edge of your seat. It will keep you wanting more, more, and more.

Acknowledgements

I give praises for an excellent family, and a loyal and faithful husband who explores the life of an addicted woman who didn't realize or care about no one, not even herself. This is my story with an interesting concept with unforgettable characters. This story is woven with true events that will keep you wanting more. I thank God for getting me over the rocky parts, as well as my husband, family, and friends for their unfailing support. This book that I have written is such an inspiration to me. I would like to give thanks to my loving God above who kept me, and my wonderful husband who stayed on me at all times and for supporting me through it all. I would like to give thanks to my sisters Beatrice Clark and Brenda Pearson for believing in me, also my great brother-in-law for letting me know that I could really do all things through Christ that strengthens me despite all I went through to get here. Thanks David Pearson, my brother-in-law for bringing the family together and telling them to get me home with a serious mind to do so. Again I would like to say thanks to You God, my Heavenly Father, my husband, sisters, and friends for your well doings.

I saw myself as camera would and often thought of myself as a sick person. As if an omniscient eye were looking down on me and my activities. I was extremely different from the rest of my family members. I talked to myself out loud. I pictured myself as wanting to be like my other siblings. I was the only one out of seven girls and four boys who felt like the black sheep of the family meaning I was different from the rest. My life coming up as a child was more than great. I was what you would call to her mother the *golden child*. Growing up, the older siblings had to pull wood, take out the waste buckets; things that now we don't have to do anymore. Now we can go to the restroom and flush the waste away. I had the mind of a genius, very smart in school, played in all different types of sports that I could and was good at it. I was always awarded with certificates, trophies, and medals that you could look back at when you got older and be proud of the things that would inspire you to want to continue to do good in life. I had a child at the age of fifteen and you would think that this would hold back the average teenager, well not in my case. My mother took the child and I continued to pursue my education. I graduated with honors. My mother had a tutor to come into our home during the time of my pregnancy to make sure I kept up with my classmates. I went on with my life very well until my mother took sick with breast cancer and was no longer able to take care of me and my child. My father was in the home but my mother was the one that always spoke up. I got caught up in the game of drugs and alcohol somewhere along the time after my first marriage failed. I began to give into the drug life that was more than I could imagine. I had an older sister to step in by the name of Gloria. She was just the meaning of her name: Glory. There was a time I could remember when she walked outside and the family was all sitting under this big tree that we had in our yard where everyone would come and sit around and drink beer, smoke pot, doing things that was not obedient as far as the law was concerned. Gloria walked up and noticed the look in my eyes. She asked me to come over and let her see why my eyes were looking so weak. That was when the first lie was told. I said to her that there's nothing wrong with me. Leave me alone. Gloria shouted out with the loudest tone I've ever heard from her, she said "Girl if you don't get over here, I am coming to get you." And when she spoke, she meant every word that came out of her mouth. Oh boy you better move or you would not like what was coming next. I knew she meant what she said and knowing that I was on drugs, I didn't have the time to argue, so I ran away from her that day. At that time nothing really mattered to me. I was not aware of the things that I was doing to myself and really I didn't care. Later, other family members started to notice a change. Thinking I could outsmart my family, I started using excuses saying that I was going to the club. By me being so spoiled, I could always have my way. This was not hard to do at all, especially when you are on addictive drug such as crack cocaine. It becomes very easy to tell a lie because this drug is a mood altering drug. It's Satan himself and from experience, I can really tell you from firsthand knowledge that telling lies, conning, scheming, stealing, and getting away quickly from a situation is not very hard to do. So when my family members started to notice a change in me, they had no idea I was even using this drug, it became real easy to lie about anything. My mother noticed that I was not coming home as usual. Every time I came into the house, I would lock my car up because this is where I kept all my paraphernalia inside of my glove box. I started coming into the house at all different times of the night and that was strange to my mother. I began sleeping all day and my moods became different. You couldn't say but a few things to me and I would fly off the handle. I started going to this club where everyone hung out. Back then I had the figure of a model that some would call a young tenderoni. I ran into this man that was a lot older and more experienced than me. His way of having fun was totally different. I remind you here I have a brand new Nissan Sentra that was purchased off the truck with zero miles on it; that's how spoiled my mother had me. Well this man knew my brother Kelvin very well. Ridley was so handsome to me, I asked my brother Kelvin to introduce me to Ridley and without any further questions, and it was done. Now I didn't know that Ridley was drug dealer, but Kelvin knew what this man was all about. Unfortunately, this was where my first drug experience started. One day, I saw my brother and his friend Ridley put some white powdery substance up their noses. They would lean back their heads and sniff this stuff up their nose. I started to ask questions one day to my brother and Ridley knew if I said anything. I would not get a chance to be around them anymore. I never spoke a word to anyone of what I had seen. I started to see more of Ridley. He was so popular, he drove around in this nice Mustang and I loved nice cares. I felt if a guy had a nice car that was the happening. This car had dark tinted windows, five star rims, and a paint job that would hurt your eyes to look at it. Life was so confusing to me at this time; I rushed into marriage at the age of eighteen to my daughter's father that didn't turn out so well. I was abused very badly and mistreated by his family. At times, if I didn't do certain things for certain family members then I was a problem. I felt I would not be accepted into a family I started to feel so nasty for especially with all the things I had to put up with. I really couldn't take it anymore; I felt that his family's mistreatment of me had a lot to do with the way my mindset started to be at such a young age. To deal with my problems, I went to see Ridley, my brother's friend, who seemed like the only person that would listen and understand me. He genuinely acted like he was concerned about me; however, as time went on, I realized that he caught me at a vulnerable time in my life and took advantage of me. It seemed to me like love at first sight but the whole time, he was out looking for another victim to pull into his world of sin. We were all sitting around after I had been abused again by my husband and his brothers on this cold night in October. I mentioned this to Ridley and he went out to get some beers for us to drink. When he got back, not only did he have the beer, but he pulled out this bag with this powdered substance in it. I wondered if this powder was the same powder I had been seen him and my brother Kelvin using to put up their nose on several occasions. Ridley told me that if I tried this, all my worries and troubles would be forgotten. I asked him are you sure about this? How could this little bag of stuff end all of my problems? He kept saying just go on and try it, but I refused at least three times that night. After he kept giving me beer after beer, twelve in total, I was starting to feel sick but good at the same time. It's what you would call drunk but I was still able to focus. Ridley told me after I started crying and repeating myself about all that had happened to me that if I just take one snort, all of my troubles would be over. Ridley was a ladies' man. All of the women wanted him and I really wanted him to like me so I gave it a try. Upon my first try of the drug, my nose pooled with blood. I jumped out of his car so fast and got into mind and sped off quickly to go home and it seemed like nothing really happened. My problems was still in my mind as I laid in the bed staring at the ceiling all night. Whatever he had given me definitely wouldn't let me go to sleep until after 4 am. The next morning I felt myself going to sleep after my heart finally slowed down. It felt like my heart was beating like a base drum on a marching band. The next day I woke up miserable with a hangover. My mother came into the room and asked me did I want anything to eat. I immediately refused. Just the sound of the word food made me sick. I went to take a shower hoping that would make me feel better and it did. I decided to call Ridley up because I didn't want him to think I was just a young girl who couldn't do grown up things. After our phone conversation, we made plans to meet later that night at the club in this small community called Middle Six. We both go there at seven p.m. just as we had planned on the phone earlier that morning. I saw my brother Kelvin there and he came up to Ridley's car and handed him some money. In exchange, Ridley gave him a small bag. Kelvin left Ridley's car and came over to my car, opened the door, and sat with me. We talked and laughed about the night before when my nose was bleeding and my hangover from all of the drinking. Ridley's first real conversation with me was centered on me trying this drug. He kept insisting that I should I should try it again, and practically guaranteed me that my nose wouldn't bleed this time. I hesitated for a while. I said let's drink a few beers first, and we went into the club and ordered beer until I was beginning to feel tipsy. After a lot of dancing and clubbing, Ridley went over to his car. He had a small amount of drugs in a bag he kept pulling out the whole time we was in the club. After he kept leaving and coming back, I assumed people were purchasing this stuff that's supposed to be so good and make you forget all your worries. We sat in Ridley's car and after much persistence on his part, I decided to give this drug he kept trying to give me another try. My nose didn't bleed this time and there didn't seem to be any effect from it. Ridley asked me would I like to go to my cousin's house who I hadn't seen in a long time. I said that sounds good to me. When we got there I recognized my first cousin James and lots of other people sitting around a table. At first I thought they were playing cards but what they had going on had nothing to do with cards. There were pipes all over the table and smoke in the air. I immediately asked Ridley what they were doing. He said this is the same as what me and you just did but they smoke theirs. This is what we do when we run out of powder, Ridley said to me. Come on it's the same. You will love it. I promise you'll forget all about your troubles so believing what he said, I was down for it. This is where it all started at my cousin James' house in the little community called Middle Six. Ridley was my main man and crack cocaine was my way of forgetting troubles. The job that I working on was not of importance to me. All I wanted then was to find Ridley and get what I needed. The following Monday was a work day. Oh was it hard to get up and go to work. In order to keep my family from believing anything different, I had to go to work. Well the money I was making on my job just seemed to be enough for my habit because when Friday came, my money was spent so fast supporting my drug habit that it seemed as if I was working for no reason. So I decided to talk to Ridley and see was there something different I could do to earn more wages. He assured me it was no problem and told me I didn't need to go back to work. Ridley said as young and pretty as you are, I'll hook you up and you can sit at James' house and sell this for me indicating a big quantity of cocaine in the powder form and some was in rock. I began to get nervous so I asked James was it just that easy and he replied girl quit acting like a little girl and do as I say. Do you want to make more money or go back to that piece of shit job and bring home three hundred dollars a week? Well I knew working at my regular job was not giving me enough money to support my habit so I thought I would try to sell these drugs. I met Ridley at James' house the next morning around seven. I noticed that James and a lot more people were there. In fact these were the same people from the night before and everyone seemed to have on the same clothes. I asked Ridley why everyone was still dressed the same way as the day before. His attitude started to change. He began to get upset with me every time I asked a question. He replied to me with a very angry tone, stop being so damn nosey and just do as I say! I didn't want to make him mad, so I listened to what he said when we went into James's house. We sat in the front room while the others were in the kitchen sitting around the table. Ridley started to count large amounts of money out of his pocket that was all rumpled up; this was more than I had ever seen at one time in a person's pocket. He reached into this little purple bag he was carrying and pulled out a lot of small bags of cocaine. Within this bag, there were around twelve bags of cocaine and about ten bags of marijuana. He handed it to me, he said that this stuff is bagged up in twenties and it's not to sell for anything less than that. If they don't have all of the money you don't give it to them. He handed me a cell phone. I was given the number to the cell phone and instructed to call him if I had any problems out of anyone; if I did he would be there before I could blink my eyes. I started to feel a little safer than I felt, although I didn't believe Ridley really cared, he was just concerned about getting his money. I was under the impression that I would at least make more money than I was making off my job. Before he left, he reached into his front pocket and handed me a small bag and told me that this was for me to smoke if I got the urge to do some. We sat around and started to mingle. He let everyone especially James, the owner of the house, know what was going on. They walked off and talked for quite some time. Standing over by Ridley's car, James came into the house and assured me that nothing was going to happen to me and not to sell to anyone I didn't recognize. James told me to ask him if I had any questions about how to do all the things that I was uncomfortable about doing. By midday, people started to pour in. By then, Ridley had left and said he would be checking in with me from time to time. If I needed him just call. I was feeling very uneasy because people that knew my brother started to ask questions like you got a brother named Kelvin? He was well known by his addiction, and I wasn't even thinking that he might show up to buy as well. Business was doing well until I started to feel hungry. On my regular job, I would usually eat a doughnut and grab a cup of coffee. Well this day was different because I didn't eat anything at all. The only thought I had was to get money for Ridley but little did I know he wasn't concerned about my overall wellbeing. He said he would be back to check on me but he never did. When he did call, he was only concerned about money and never would say anything about what I needed. He seemed to not care whether or not things were okay with me or not. At about 1:30pm, I met some ladies that I thought were cool. My thought process was I could hang around this crowd of ladies and become popular. I met this older lady by the name of Sara. She had to be every bit fifty years old and I mentioned Ridley and shared with her some of the things that I was trying to do with him. Sara told me that I was a fool and every time she would hit that pipe she would tell me how foolish I was to mess with Ridley. She even told me he had a wife and 12 kids; how he has brought lots of women out there and they were doing the same thing that I was doing for him. I tried to ignore most of her conversation because I knew these women didn't seem normal to me. I tried to change the subject and tell her that I was hungry and she proceeded to tell me about how this rock would stop all things including hunger and pain. She said once she had a toothache and she didn't have to go to the dentist. She just took her a hit of rock cocaine and all her pain went away that instant. Me and Sara became very close. She was a professional liar and she was teaching me how to be one also. I was well trained by this lady. Me and her sat there and began to smoke until I was all out and with nothing on my stomach, I started to feel sick so I called Ridley. When he answered, his first question was are you sold out or do you need more? I was starting to see what Sara was trying to tell me all along. Even though she was looking like she didn't have good sense, she really did know all the ropes to this game. Not only was Sara a great liar, she was prostitute well known all over town. Ridley was taking too long to come back to the house and Sara and I needed some more drugs. She decided to take me to this house down the street. When this man came to the door, she asked him was his wife at home. He said his wife was at work. He responded back to come on in. This guy looked so familiar to me. He said his name was Jimmy. When he called me by my name, I immediately asked him how he knew my name. He told me not to worry about that and started to come on to me very strong. This lady who I tried to start a friendship with was also a pimp. She was pimping me to this guy. They went into the room and talked for a couple of minutes. I could not understand what they were saying but it was not long before they both returned. Jimmy told me to come on back so we could talk. When we got into the room he never asked me how old I was, in fact he never gave me a chance to say anything. He began taking off all his clothes and asked me to do all these disgusting things to him for twenty dollars. He said he had already paid Sara for this business transaction that I was supposed to be handling, and I had better stick to my part of the deal. I was so high and confused and awfully sick, so I went along with what he told me to do. I was only a hundred pounds and this guy was at least four hundred pounds. I was so afraid of this guy, especially with the tone of voice he was using; I didn't know how this was going to play out. When everything was over I left and never saw which way Sara had gone. I went home and the next day I saw James. He was really mad at me for going home so early from day before. Initially, we were to me at the spot to get more product to make more money. I was so ashamed after he had found out what I had done with my body by prostituting myself. I was the talk of the town. Ridley could not believe what he was hearing that this lady had pimped me out for money. I was more hurt about it than anything, mainly because I had found out that my cousin had recognized me but didn't try to stop this. I was so mad at myself after Ridley said so many hurtful words to me calling me everything except a child of God. After his tirade, I decided I would go home. This plan didn't go as I thought it would. Ridley wanted his money for the product that me and Sara had smoked. She was nowhere to be found and I had to have this money by dark and Ridley didn't care where I got it from, all he wanted was his money. He started to tell me how everything that goes on he knows about, even if he's asleep in his bed. So I knew then that he had people working for him that didn't mind telling him what he needed to know to get what they wanted. He started to talk to me like I was just a street person telling me that all this came with the game. I started to cry. Ridley told me to suck it up and get his damn money. I ran to my car. He screamed out to me saying don't make me come looking for you. That is when I found out all this was just a game to him. I gave Ridley his money by the time night fell. I went home and told my parents a lie about my car and got the money. I returned to James' house where Ridley was and gave him the money. Quickly, I gave him his money, got in my car and left. The next following day, I tried to call Ridley but he never answered the phone. I had tried to return to work but there was no job for me because I had been fired. My boss told me that he had to replace me for not calling in and he had no other choice but to terminate me. He needed a secretary to get his work out for that day or he was going to be fired. I went home and told my mother that I had gotten laid off from my job. That was the biggest lie that could ever be told. I had been fired for not calling or coming in. I didn't want to be a disappointment to my mother and father so I kept lying. I knew now that I had really messed up so I got on the phone and called Ridley. Luckily, he answered the phone for me. I explained to him that I really needed to see him about making some money. He said he would meet me at James' house at seven that evening. Me and Ridley talked things over and I was back in the game selling drugs and I was promised to have all I wanted to smoke and drink. Just make the bread he said and I knew he really meant what he said. I was told if I liked to live, I better do the right thing with this package. I started leaving home every morning going to James' house everyday making money and getting high. I was introduced to a lot of people that I had never seen in my life. Some of these people were big drug dealers from Columbia, SC and some were local people from the area. Everybody was in this for the money and they made it clear not to play with their money or it was not going to be nice. I felt I really had it going on now I had all the money I needed and all the drugs I needed to smoke. Best of all Ridley and I started to get back close. I was now feeling important to him because I was making a lot more money than he was. I knew now that he really needed me just as much as I needed him. As I got deeper into my drug usage, people who knew my family started to notice me and what I was doing. The news had even reached my parents. I was starting to party so much until I was not thinking about paying my bills anymore including my car insurance to lapse. I would go by the house every now and again to get my mail and this is when I found out that my car was getting repossessed and that the insurance was terminated. I met this guy named Carl that was selling drugs while Ridley was out doing his thing and I was telling him about my problems. Again I got close to another man. He suggested to me that he could help me. All I had to do was look good for the guys when they came in the door, make them spend money with him, and he would pay my car insurance and my car payment. This went on and things were good until my family found out where I was. They found out because Carl's sisters knew my sisters from school. The word got out real fast. My mother and sisters came looking for me in this small town called Ridgeway, SC. Once they found me, they took me right on to rehab. They saw how poorly my face looked and realized instantly that something was wrong. My mother took the car and returned it back to the dealership since I wouldn't be able to afford it any longer considering the condition I was in. My family had decided they wouldn't be financially responsible with paying for a car that I was using to go get drugs in. I stayed in rehab in Winnsboro, SC for two weeks and I found out how to get out without anyone knowing and that's what I did. I escaped out the back door since there was no security. Rehab allowed anyone to walk around as they saw fit. I left and was walking up the street seeking out the dope houses. My knowledge of these locations came from delivering drugs from Ridley. I thought I knew my way around really well. I even knew how not to be found if I didn't want to be found. This young guy in this really nice car picked me up on Ward One, another popular location for drugs. This guy asked me did I need a ride. I quickly responding yes hoping no one saw me get into this car. This man was really ugly and fat; definitely someone I wouldn't be seen with in public. I really needed some money for dope and I also needed a place to hide out before my family was onto me. I was completely honest with this guy and told him I needed money to get high with. He asked me do you mess with that shit. I replied sometimes and I am in need right now so don't start with me. He said to each his own and told me he sold what I needed. I told him that I didn't have any money. He said "that's okay, I guess I have a little bit you can try." That's all I wanted to hear. As we were driving around, I told him all about myself and what I had gotten into. Listening to my story made him want to take care of me. He even suggested that he might be able to help me get off drugs. He told me that I was too pretty and young to be on that shit. I told him if I had to listen to that, just leave me alone. Right now I don't need that; that's why I left the hospital so I could do as I pleased. This guy went and got a motel room right located right beside the jail and that really had me scared, but it didn't stop me from smoking my crack cocaine and nothing was going to get in my way In my mind, I was my own woman and I could do as I pleased. Me and this guy started to get close only because he had what I wanted. Since he had never had sex before, I knew then that I had me a sucker for the road. All I had to do was to teach him the ropes about sex and I could get him to anything I wanted and that's exactly what I did. I got him hooked on me and he started to give me all the drugs I wanted and he would make sure I had it or I would not give him any sex. I couldn't go nowhere without him wanting to go along and that started to make me mad. He asked if he get us a house, would I feel better. I said yes and that's what he did. He went and got us a mobile home and paid cash for it. I knew that he had to have started getting bigger in the game. I had given him all my old connections and he started to get the big head. He started to abuse me if I didn't do what he wanted done and that was different because I never had a guy hit me before. He became so big in the game that the feds were onto him and eventually he got arrested. I never knew how deep he was into the game since he always walked around like he didn't have a pot to piss in or a window to throw it out of. He had the local police thinking the same as me. After he left and got sentenced, I moved back home. Shortly after that my mother passed and I was really up shit creek. I had to really do for myself now so I moved to Columbia with my uncle. He passed after three years of me being there. Before moving in with my uncle, things had gotten pretty bad with this man I decided I would stay with. The longer we stayed together, the worst things got so he decided in order to keep up my habit, and he would sell drugs to support my habit. We would go up and down the road to cop the drugs from different people. Things went well for awhile until he started to get bigger in the game. Things went well for a while until he decided he would give me just enough drugs to control me and make me want more. This arrangement went on for a while until he realized what drugs could get women to do for it. He concluded that by using drugs to get women to do any and every thing for that high was better than getting money from the ones that was really addicted to it. All of a sudden, he stopped giving me the way that he used to. Things really went from sugar to shit. I started going to different places where people my age would never hang out at, such as the club called the OFJ. Oh, I really would have good time in that place. I had gotten enough money to get my own car even though my mother and father had me spoiled rotten. I had things most kids my age did not have so I held a higher advantage. I had two kids Shada and Artreso, who were being raised by my mother so coming home early was not a problem for me. This worked for a little while until my mother got tired of my smart ways and me taking advantage of her. I thought since I had kids, I had outgrown physical punishment such as spanking. When my mother had enough of me coming in at all times of the night, I thought she was trying to kill me when she whipped me. No way would I have ever thought that my mother would have the strength to beat me that bad. I started to scream and hollering for my mama to stop. She had just decided she would give me exactly what I needed. I called myself getting mad at my mom and decided I would show her a thing or two, so I started hiding out in places where no one would find me. I started going with men twice my age to get things I wanted. I really could get those old guys to give me whatever my heart desired. I started out with this older man by stealing his checkbook. That was the first time I had ever went to jail, well my mother found me then. She was the first one I called when this happened,

I started t o run with drug dealers. I got a charge of strong armed robbery and distribution. I didn't really care whether I got out of this or not. I needed to rest anyway. My oldest sister came to rescue me in spite of my poor decisions. My mom was diagnosed with cancer. My sister told me that mom was real sick and I needed to straighten up my act. Well as you know that went in one ear and out the other. I knew my mother's illness was getting worse and she wouldn't be able to run behind me anymore, so now I guessed it was up to my remaining sisters to do it. I wasn't really worried about my brothers because I thought they didn't really care about what I did, at least they didn't appear to seem concerned. I was so mean and crazy on them drugs, I guess they just didn't want to have to hurt me by the way I was acting. My mother soon passed away with cancer. I started to feel like I was the reason for it, I had to now take my two kids and do what real women were suppose to do. My oldest sister came and rescued me again. She saw where there was no way I could see after my own kids by the way I was living. I didn't know how to take care of myself. I was getting in so much trouble that none of my family wanted nothing to do with me. The department of social services had decided they would take my kids if I didn't stay out of trouble. That still didn't do me any good. My baby brother paid out a lot of money to get my kids to stay with my oldest sister. He had to spend a lot of money on an attorney. I went right on in the street and caught a murder charge for something I had nothing to do with. You think that would change a person but with me it seemed to get worst after my oldest sister got me out of that mishap where the criminal charges were dismissed. That monster named cocaine had a hold on me that no one could break loose. I was thrown in rehab and I did good for six months and returned back on the loose. After I knew my sister had my kids, I decided I would come home when I was ready. My family knew I had a serious problem. I would always throw up in my sister's face you all know what Mommy told ya'll to do. I was still the baby. They all knew that but they was so fed up with me if they could have killed me and gotten away with it, I think they would have because I was nothing that my family expected I would be. Eventually, I became involved with another guy who wanted me to do things that I really didn't want to do. We started to stay together and all the time, he would tell me how to go out and get this drug called cocaine by any means necessary. I wanted this guy so much; I did these things at his request. After I told him how hot the police were out there on the other girls and how they were being arrested for prostitution. Once he made threats to me to leave me and get other girls, I pleaded with him that I would do anything for him; just tell me and he did and I started to do exactly what he wanted me to do. I started to date other people, not to say that I was in love with anyone because at this time I didn't love myself. So when I started to get with these other guys, they became my tricks. Tricks are defined by guys who would pay for sexual services rendered in a short period of time. This was just my way of getting money to support my huge habit. This man started to beat every guy I would talk to. He acted like he had never touched a woman in his entire life. This man started to kidnap me. He had really gotten out of hand with this situation between me and him and I didn't know what to do or who to turn to about what was going on. After the money was not what he wanted it to be, I would run away from this man. He would always find me and take me to these weird places where no one could find me and do what he wanted to do to me. He was not a bad looking guy, its just that all the other women knew him and his mean ways toward women. They started to tell me and I would push them away. He was telling me how he could get other women but he didn't feel comfortable with them. He was taking my body every time he caught up to me in the streets. He knew that I was not the street type, that I was a country girl that didn't know anything about the streets so this is where he had me. He knew all the street games and how to trap the innocent ones who was very afraid and naïve to the game. After things got so bad, I was in and out of jail trying to learn the streets. I begged him to please find someone else to do this for him and let me go free. He agreed with me but as time went on, three months later, he found me inside of a crack house and decided he would try his old games again. We started to talk and by me being as addicted to this drug the way, I was wanted what he had and he had what I wanted. So wet got this thing back to rolling again. We started to see each other again and this went on good for about two weeks, and then he started to go back to his old ways. He started to get real aggressive with me toward everything I knew, and then we were right back where we started from, in an abusive relationship. He had started to ask people what I was doing and had they seen me around even when I tried to hide from him. He had started that old mess again looking and threatening people to tell him exactly where I was. If they didn't give him the answer he wanted, he would threaten to do harm to them. He eventually found me in this house I was in at the moment and kicked down the door. I was so afraid as he grabbed me and he was asking everyone in the house did they want some too. He was continuously making threats telling them that they could get some to indicating a beat down that he was sure to give me. When are at bugged out the way I was on crack until you are silent for the affects this drug is causing you, paranoia and numbness sets in. This guy beat me for at least five minutes and no one in the house took a thing to do with it. This man had everyone in the neighborhood afraid of him. I was beaten so badly until I could see nothing but darkness. My so called friends didn't have the decency to call the police or even try to stop me from getting beaten up. They were so cracked out; I don't even think they could have done anything considering the condition they were in. He grabbed me and took me to this cemetery where he had already dug the grave for me. He told me that he was going to bury me alive that if he couldn't have me then no one would. He held my mouth with a strong grip and forced pills into my mouth. He held my throat until the pills were all gone. I started to feel myself get drowsy and when I woke up I was in a motel room and he was standing there crying telling me how much he loved me. I found out later he had given me sleeping pills knowing he could have killed me. He didn't care, he was just that devious. He was so coldhearted towards me; I thought being with no one else but him mattered until he was willing to take a chance on ending my life. When I did finally woke up I found that I was in Blythewood, SC and it was Christmas Day. I had gone through Christmas Eve being beaten half to death. I was involved with this guy and he started to do things to me that no one with their right mind would have dealt with. I was not attracted to this guy at all; he was just selling the stuff I wanted and I made him feel like he was on top of the world. The situation got so bad with me and this guy I could remember how he took me from a friend's house. This guy alongside his brother kicked my friend's door in and grabbed me. I was not aware of this big arrival and what was going to happen next. Just close your eyes and imagine this happening to you or just anyone for that matter when the door was kicked in and I was dragged to his car. His brother got in the back seat and he was driving. The entire time he was driving I was being hit and beaten repeatedly over and over again in my face with the back his hand. He was screaming at me did you really think you could get rid of me just that easy Bitch! When we got to this place in the woods where they had planned out to do whatever they were going to do to me, it was a cemetery where they had already dug the hole to put me in. I was so afraid. He had this thing for cemeteries where he would always take me to when he became angry at me. I really thought this time it would be over for me. His brother received a call and had to leave so we went to drop his brother off and he continued to drive towards the Shell Station in Winnsboro. It just had to be God because he needed gas. He decided to untie me and I started to tell him that I loved him and we could work thinks through. I declared to him I would never leave him again or never do anything to hurt him. I could tell he was falling for this so when we got to the gas station, he decided he would let me go to the bathroom. Once I got inside, I had to ask the gas attendant for the key to the restroom. When I was close enough to the cashier, I started to tell her that I was kidnapped. Immediately she called the police. When the police arrived they blocked the car in and threw him to the ground. When I got to the police station, I was so swollen; I barely could get my words out. The young lady that called was around my age and I remembered her from school. We used to drive the buses together; I was really thanking her for coming to the police station and testifying to what she had seen. I was then transported to the police station for tests to be run. I was asked al lot of questions about what occurred. My report to the police had to be honest is all the officer stated over and over again. I told the officer that I would be afraid of his brother finding me if I told them everything. They assured me they were going to go after him so fast that he wouldn't have time to find me. They finished up with me at the hospital late that night. The officers transported me to the station so I could make an official statement and that's exactly what they did. This guy was charged with kidnapping, assault and battery, and rape. His brother was charged with kidnapping, assault with intent to kill, and conspiracy to rape. When I was told I could leave the station, I called my friend, the one whose door was kicked in to get me. My friend immediately came to get me; we went back to his place. He had fixed everything back the way it was supposed to be. The next day he had to make a statement of what he had witnessed to the police. I tried to move on with my life but the guys who kidnapped and assaulted me had their mother and grandmother hunting me down like I was a dog. Every time I went into town, people were telling me I needed to get in touch with these women. They sought me out with such urgency; I began staying at home a lot more, feeling like they wanted me something bad. I stopped hanging in certain places that I used to hoping they would get off my trail. After a month had passed by, I thought all of this was over, but to my dismay the mother and grandmother was at my door crying and it all started to make me feel guilty. I felt like I had done something wrong to them when I was the victim. They both laid this guilt trip on me persuading me both of these men were good people. I stated to his grandmother what had happened to me and she started screaming that her chest was hurting like she was going to have a heart attack. I felt so sorry for her; she really was a sweet old lady; however, I later found out from him, in a heated argument, that she was just faking me out to get me to drop the charges. One week later I decided to ride with the mother and grandmother to the court house and speak with the solicitor to drop the charges. This was all over now and I felt I could get back to my own business. Nothing mattered but getting money to support my habit. Since the charges had been dropped, this guy stayed away and I really had time to party. I moved into my family's house all by myself and there was no one to tell me what to do or how to do it. I could stay out all night if I wanted to. I was just going and coming as I please bringing who I wanted to into the house. When I would go to other family member's homes, who lived close by, they really didn't mess with me figuring all I wanted was a cigarette or beer or money. I quickly became the least favorite person to be around. These family members never came down to the house to see me because of my attitude. This is just one of the many consequences of using drugs, isolation from family members. I would stay up all night chasing crack cocaine and was not getting any sleep. During the day, I would sleep, and like the old saying goes, the freaks come out at night. A freak: this is what I was known as to the older guys in the neighborhood who knew what my habit was. Knowing this, they would come around for a little fun for a small fee. I don't think my family members who lived close by knew what these old guys were really up to. Come to think of it, only distant relatives knew what kind of life I lived and what I was addicted to. By now, life for me wasn't so bad; I had learned how to deal with not having as much by getting a quick fix, and still go out to the clubs and hustle more. I prided myself with keeping up with my personal hygiene. I knew nobody wanted to deal with someone stinky and ugly. The drugs would always have me where I thought I had an odor. Other addicts would smell bad, and I didn't want to be that way not caring what I smelled or looked like. I guess it had a lot to do with the way I was brought up. I started to hang at the corner store in the neighborhood where I grew up. This was a place where all the drunks, addicts, and men who wanted to have a good time would be at. I would bring them all to my house to get what I wanted. I went to the same corner store one night and was not looking for no man to call my own when I met this good looking guy. He had a nice ride and he was looking for a good time. We got together and went to his house. He had no idea about my habit and I kept that a secret. This gentleman looked like someone with money, someone I didn't want to miss out on. He didn't ask much of me, just a good time that included dancing, drinking, drinking, and partying. This man loved old music and I was a music lover as well. I was actually enjoying myself and having a good time without having the high that cocaine brought me even though I would crave it, I did my best not to fall in temptation because I felt like I had a good thing going with this guy. As they say, all good things must come to an end and with that my new guy friend wanted to control me; I was definitely not used to that. I really was not ready to slow down even though I liked this guy. The drugs were still calling my name we had made a decision to move in together which turned out to be a big mistake. Honestly, I was not ready for this and having the wild life style that I was living. He dealt with my foolishness for a while. I felt he was going to eventually catch me, so I chose to leave while he was at work. This man's feelings hard started to change towards me and that scared me. I thought he might even kill me.

Everyone knew of his reputation and from what I heard I didn't want no part of. My whole life back then was a façade; I wanted to get what I could and move on. It was even better if I could get someone to take care of me which made me happy. It didn't matter to me what this person looked or smelled like just as long as he could give me what I wanted when I wanted it. This was really a good man but I started to feel like I needed space and that's what I did. I went back to my home in my own place where I could start back doing the things I used to do with the same people I was used to having around me. I continued supplying my habit and I was at peace. Time went on and I started to hang at this crack house in Winnsboro, SC. There, I met this guy who appeared to not be addicted to crack but he did like to smoke weed. We got to talking and I was telling him how I had my own place in Simpson and he became very interested in me, not knowing he was shooting me a bunch of bullshit. He just needed a place to lay his head; come to find out he was on crack worst then me. Together our crack habit totaled $100 per day. One day, I just got tired of getting high off this drug. My body was shutting down after so many days of getting high. Your body will start to shut down by itself and you really can't do anything but go to sleep or have a heart attack. To anyone who knows about this drug can relate to what I am talking about. You keep on and on and when your body starts to tell you to go to sleep, your heart starts to pound so bad until you can place your hand on your chest and feel the effects of this drug called crack cocaine. This guy I was dealing with did not really know what he was getting himself into. We were on the roller coaster ride of drugs for weeks until things started to get real bad for us. I was not staying home; I was wherever I could get that next fix for me and my new so called lover. The bills that I had to pay in the house was not that much, mainly the utility bill. I had gotten to the point where I didn't want to pay that anymore. I was always trying to keep up with him in the streets. With him not doing what he was suppose to do as a man, things were really hard. He wanted me to do things that I was not proud of to get money while he waited on me to come back to him with the funds get high and pay bills. He would make all sorts of crazy threats and me not having enough sense to be afraid of what this guy what capable of doing, I would be ready to battle. One day, I decided I would leave and go to town and do what I needed to do. I was so hungry this day; I had sold all of my food stamps so we didn't know where our next meal was going to come from. He decided he would get his nerves up to tell me that he was in love with me. He started to block me from talking to guys that wanted to help me, but as time went on I seemed to get myself into more and more trouble with this guy. Truthfully, I have always made bad choices in life when it came to a man and relationships. They always seemed to be the ones who didn't want anything in life and wanted to use me and beat me in the end. This guy had me going to jail more and more. In time, I caught a charge along with him which scared me; I thought I would never see daylight again. I caught a murder charge fooling around with this guy. I was so frightened when the police questioned me about things I never heard of before. I was being threatened by the police officers to talk or I would be there for the rest of my life. I was being railroaded. I was only twenty three when I got this charge. They started to ask me questions about drug dealers that I refused to answer, and then I was charged with strong arm robbery and conspiracy to distribution. I told them I didn't know what they were talking about, so eventually they found out the truth and my charges were dismissed. Unbeknownst to me, this guy I was dating was dating was murderer. He came back later to confess to me what he had done and right then and there I called the police. All this time, it seemed as thought I was in out and of jail for years. After this last incident, I went back to the house I grew up in. I had gotten myself into so many abusive relationships you would think I was Joe Frazier's sister. I did not learn how to fight by growing up or from kids I grew up with in my neighborhood, but from these abusive relationships with guys who wished to control me. I tried to keep a lot of secrets in my relationships because I had a lot of serious charges and really nobody would trust you as a murderer or a strong armed robber. I met this guy that was willing to go to court with me and a lot of things came out that he didn't know and in the long run it was thrown in my face. I ended up getting another charge for cutting him that still didn't help any. He was still up and down the road wanting to be with me, so now I had to become real good at what to do in a bad relationship. Instead of the men beating me, it got to the point I started being the gangster. I had started to look so bad, people that hadn't seen me in a while was asking me what was going on with me. I just politely said nothing but knowing in my heart, fighting plus beating plus using drugs equals death and ugliness. People who looked at me wrong made me feel they were out to get me, and I started to feel like a lion protecting her cubs. I would start an argument not knowing or caring if I would get killed in the process. I had gotten into so much trouble that the police knew me by name in my hometown so I decided I would move to Columbia with my Uncle. He was my mother's brother; he had done a decade of time in the penitentiary and was out on parole.

Sitting outside, me and my brother would drink our cold beers on the weekend. I really didn't have to worry too much about how I would get some beer to drink. People always would stop by with beer on the weekend just to have someone to shoot the jive with. My brother Raymond could jive with anyone very well. If you were the type that didn't like to be teased then you should never come around him the neighborhood. On one said occasion, my Uncle thought he would call it like he saw it. He said to me calling me by my nickname, "Lirie you look older than me and I am eight years old." Everyone that was around started to laugh at what my uncle said. I had a temper and it wasn't good for anyone to say too much to me. My temper was a consequence of using drugs especially when you couldn't get high. My uncle continued to talk to everyone else as if I was not there. I became very quiet, and my brother called me into the house to give me a little history of how our Uncle had spent life in the penitentiary for killing a man and child. I guess he tried to spook me but it really didn't make any difference to me what he had done. I was still not afraid of anything. I used to hear all the stories my mama would talk about how her brother didn't care anything about doing harm to people and how quick his temper was. Listening to the many stories about my uncle made me think this was maybe where I got some of my don't-care-attitude from. I use to think for a while that everyone hated me especially when I would express my feelings. My uncle decided he would come into the house where I was to talk to me. He sat down and started to tell me things that he had been through in his life. At the time I was so addicted to crack cocaine and so hard headed, when he was speaking these things to me I was totally ignoring him. To me I would just say yes in a very sarcastic way until he started to notice that I was the one that was out of control. I was so far gone that I needed someone to really care, but have a firm grip on me and to love me with emphasis on the love part. After he saw how

25

I really was, he asked me to go back to Columbia with him where he resided. He told me that he could use me around his place to help do things that he would pay me to do. This sounded good to me; however, I didn't know where I would get my crack. I knew I had a cousin that was staying there that used also and that was where I would find out about my connections. My uncle started out by giving me fifty dollars to drive him to visit with other family members. I knew this was going to be good day for me because to an addict fifty dollars is just like having a million dollars or hitting the jackpot. He told me to make sure I showered and put on some good looking clothes. I did just that and my life in Columbia began. When I got there, his wife, Aunt Ann, just fell in love with me. I said to myself this is working out in my favor. As time went on, my cousins and I would sit around and drink beer and laugh. One of my cousins who also lived there was addicted to crack cocaine. I thought by the way he looked, he had straightened his act up and was clean but boy was I wrong. All in all, I had both an alcoholic cousin and a crack addicted cousin living under the same roof. My uncle's wife Ann was an alcoholic too. This life of alcohol and drugs can lead to death and that's why all of them are dead along with some of the people that I ran with. The whole purpose of my life story is to tell others things that I saw and experienced on my own, not what someone told me. I not trying to gain financial gain, I just want to share what I went through in this honest, brutal manner giving praises to God that I was able to get out. Come to think of it, my Uncle was the only one in the house that was sober. He had a history of being an alcoholic but I assumed that prison had a lot to do with his change of life and his addiction. He would always try to tell me stories about prison; I really didn't believe the things he said he had to do to survive while incarcerated. One of the most unbelievable stories involved him letting other men perform oral sex on him to get what incentives like snacks. Things like this really do happen in prison.

He was also telling me stories of how women could come for conjugal visits but this was not enough to satisfy him. I was so lost when I moved to Columbia and my uncle's wife Ann was so mean to everyone around her until I thought to myself how in the world could anyone live here. My Uncle would slap her to the floor like she was a dog if she said anything to him that he didn't like or if she starting acting up if she had too much to drink. He would really put a beating on her so when she would start to act mean to us, we would not tell our Uncle for we feared what he would do to her. I found out real fast about that mean streak my mom would talk about that my uncle had. He would sit on the porch every day and sharpen his knife. I started to think in my mind that I wanted to get away from this house, so my cousin would always call this guy up to get drugs from him. This man would always ask him about me. I decided that the next time I saw him; I would ask him what was up with him asking about me all the time. Eventually he invited me to come by to see him. My cousin bedroom was where they made their deals at. Every time they met, our aunt would raise hell because she suspected some shady business was going on. To keep her out, we would lock the bedroom's door, do our drugs, and come out looking like really stupid. The money that my Uncle gave me for doing chores went straight to drugs. When I met a lot of other addicts around the neighborhood, I started to use more and more of this drug called crack cocaine every single day. I met my uncle's wife niece from across town when she came to visit. Little did I know we had something in common, crack cocaine. From that day forward, we decided to get together and use. On one occasion, she took me to a really, really rough part of Columbia where you could get drugs easily. All you had to do was be there and someone was bound to say something to you. This part of town was called Green Street, and this so called cousin of mine had messed with so many guys on that side of town till she had wore body out. These guys were all used to her ways and really didn't want anything to do with her. I had found my way around this part of town and knew how to get extra money. The money that my uncle was giving me was not enough to support my habit. Every day, my cousin and I wet get together for the sole purpose of getting high. My cousin had this boyfriend that I thought was more like a pimp. Every time she would go out and come back with money, she would get us some crack cocaine to smoke; but when this man she called her boyfriend would be around she would have to give him all the money. Sometimes, he would give her some of her money back. My cousin would at least have fifty dollars her, but if he was around, this money would be gone. He would get mad at her if she didn't have more money on her and make her go back up to the streets to get more. This boyfriend/pimp was verbally abusive to my cousin. I asked her why did she deal with him and the answer she gave me was that he made her feel safe and that she loved him because he would not let anything happen to her. I asked her what was all this about and she ran out the door and said that she had to go to work. I asked her to please help me get a job with her that I really needed extra money. At this request, she stopped in her tracks and said come with me now and you can start to work today. I was so excited about going to work; I figured this is what I really needed. Now I would have money for myself to get high whenever I wanted to. My cousin explained to me how this "job" worked. She told me that she would take me on the first ride with her and after that I would be on my own until I found myself a pimp. I thought that was something you only heard on television or in a movie. The first night I went out with her, I was just a young, country girl that didn't know anything about prostitution. I found out real fast what it was all about and went to jail the first night.

My uncle raised so much hell in that house when I got back home, it didn't seem like it made sense to me because they let me out without me having to pay any money, but my uncle still had to come get me since I didn't know anything about catching the bus. I went home with my Uncle and I read the papers given to me at my departure and found out that I had to appear in court. I made promises to my uncle that I would not do it again. I stayed home for five days straight. I wanted to go but I knew what I had told my Uncle. The word of an addict is nothing. When my Uncle found out what had happened and how it happened, he put my cousin out of the house and that was his wife's niece. He blamed her for all of what had happened to me. My uncle started to give me more and more money to try to keep me in the house. That was strange to me because he was just giving me money at the beginning of each month when he would get his check. This started to change things around the house. He started to ask me did I have money for that stuff that I wanted to smoke. He never would say the word crack but he knew what it was. I would always say I could always use money Unc, and he would hand me a little something to get what I wanted. I had now learned a lot of different dealers' phone numbers and would have it delivered to me so I wouldn't have to leave the house. My uncle would tell me it was okay to sit in my room and smoke. He knew how dangerous it was for me to be on those streets of Columbia, but everything that was told to me went in one ear and out the other. Some of the young dealers started to tell me that they knew my son Lil' Ru the rapper, but that was not important to me at the time. All I wanted was my product and not caring whose reputation was at state, not even my own son's. This is what this drug will do to you. They found out because my cousin went around telling people that my son was a rapper and I had not seen my kids in forever. I couldn't tell you the last time I had seen my kids. I am thinking it had to be at least ten years because my oldest sister was not about to let me come around those kids in the condition I was in. Everyone in the streets started to call me Mama Ru because of my son's stage name; that way they would know who I was when I came to their door to cop my drugs. Most things that I heard about my son were told to me from the streets. I really didn't know what was going on with my child. What he was doing with his life or his career. I had gotten in with these dealers so good that now they would just give me stuff because of who my son was. Everything seemed to be working out good in my life. My uncle started telling me to stay home to save my son's reputation. This was ludicrous to me; I really didn't want to hear none of this from him. I wanted what I wanted and that was it. Things started to get so bad with my addiction and my uncle knew this until one day he started to come into my room to ask me to do him for money. This still didn't phase me or seemed bad; actually it seemed like a good idea at the time. This is how crack cocaine works in the real world of addiction. He would tell me if I didn't, I would have to find me some place else to stay. He started locking me out of the house so I started to lay my head where I could; not thinking to I could simply go back to my hometown to stay. In Columbia, it was so easy to get drugs any time of the day or night at every corner. I had gotten myself into a lot of trouble, and there were warrants issued for my arrest, so I decided I would ask my uncle to come back home. I really hated I did that because I had to do him all the time. In exchange for performing these sexual acts, I would get paid. My uncle knew I was in a lot of trouble with the law and I didn't have any choice but live there with him. He would offer me twenty dollars every now and then whenever he felt sorry for me. My uncle would tell me just lay your body down and let me play with it. He was so old until that's all he really could do. It was just so bad for your family to treat their own flesh and blood this way without a conscience. It got so bad until I didn't care anymore. I went back out on the streets and took a chance of the police getting me and that's what happened after a week of trying to hide out. I did six months and was released back onto the streets of Columbia. Prostitutes were being killed but do you think that scared me, hell no; I wanted to see was this really true until I had to sleep one night beside a dead body thinking that the girl was sleep from running the streets for days. Soon after that, I was kidnapped and raped and beaten into a coma from the North Main murderer. Good thing I always kept a weapon on me and didn't mind using it; this is what really saved my life. I can remember cutting him deep to the point he had to seek medical attention. I really do believe I would have died then, but through it all, I still didn't stop hanging on that corner or using. When I tell you crack cocaine is a monster, will have you on a path to destruction. Please believe me. To all my readers please remember these are real life events that I am sharing so this may lead to someone else's breakthrough. Once I arrived back at my uncle's place, he decided he would go fishing. I decided to leave after having learning he and my cousin had a disagreement. I left with nothing except the clothes on my back. After about two months, I went by to see how things was going and my cousin told me that my uncle had died, and they were going to have to move out of the house. No one was able to pay the rent. I could afford to pay but I was so hurt behind all of this; at least that's what I thought I had no feelings, the only feelings I had was through that high off of dope that I so desperately sought each and every day y of my life. I didn't know how to talk to people that really cared about me. Unless you had you had what I wanted or was talking about going to get what I wanted, I had no conversation for you or what you talked about was not important to me. Not long after my Uncle passed away, Aunt Ann died in a nursing home. Word was she drunk herself into an early grave. With both my aunt and uncle gone, I had to try to survive on my own. I knew going back to my family was not an option with me and my addiction. My family definitely was not going to put up with my foolish ways and with the things I was doing, so I started to meet more people in the street and learning how to get what I needed by lying, cheating, and scheming. I knew this was not pleasing to God or the laws of the world. Once again, I started walking the streets and learning top secrets of how to get over, at least that's what I thought I was doing; however; there were a lot of people smarter than I thought. I had been in every crack house there was and tricked with every man that I could get money out of. I performed some ungodly acts but in the end I walked away with what I wanted thinking my game was on point. In the end I would find myself being beaten half the death or raped or both. I can recall one night I was walking down North Main Street, it was around four a.m. in the morning and I had just left the crack house. I had been awake for three days. I decided I would go sit on the bus stop bench to get some rest. I must have been sitting there for five minutes. No cars on the road, no people around, and this guy came up the road walking. He spoke and I spoke. This guy sat right beside me. I had no intention on even asking this man for anything. He looked like the type that didn't have anything. I had three dollars, only God knows who or where I got that money from. He began to look up and down the street like he was looking for someone so that's what I assumed he was waiting on someone. He reached into his pocket and put on a pair of dark shades; I thought he was harmless. This guy must have waited at least ten minutes to make up his mind about what he was going to do. He moved in a block position of the road. There were woods right behind us. He grabbed me and pulled me though the woods to this old abandoned house; he started to speak in a really heavy voice saying if you scream, you will die tonight in this house. It appeared to me as if someone was getting ready to move into this house. The reason I say this was because of the pretty carpet on the floor and it smelled good in there. There was no furniture anywhere, and he pulled me to the floor in a very manly way. I was so afraid. I never would pray unless it was deemed really necessary back then and this was one of those times I knew I had to pray. I started to pray silently to myself asking God to please don't end my life this way. He started to rip my clothes off and asked me to remove my pants. I didn't say a word. I remembered what some of the other girls had told me about their unpleasant experiences. I did not want to go through that so I cooperated with this man. I began to see what these girls were talking about in the crack house when they get high. I didn't believe their stories at first but they were really telling the truth, and now the time had come for me. I told him in a nice tone you don't have to do this. I love to have sex; I hadn't had a good time in a long time. We can do this without being mad or violent. He didn't respond so I could feel how light his touch had become so I started to take my clothes off willingly and he started to take his off. He began penetrating me without a condom. He started to become gentle with me and then he would masturbate and roll over like a dog. He was doing this repeatedly over and over. He told me he was going to fuck me until daylight. I said that's fine with me just let me rest a while. After a few rounds of sex, this guy became restless. I moaned and groaned to make it seem as if I was interested in him. I did whatever it took for me to stay alive. I just wanted to keep from being killed or beaten half to death. He was really doing his thing until daylight had come and I saw where he was beginning to become tired and sleep. He was so exhausted he started to fall asleep. I had a chance now to see his face. He was so drowsy because after a good orgasm, they have a tendency to fall asleep. I had a chance now to see his face and I sensed he hadn't went with a woman in long time. He fell out to sleep like a dead fly. He hadn't noticed that daylight had come in and as he started to look around, he realized that I had seen his face. He had one bad eye that looked weak; the other one was wide eyed like he had been using some type of drug. This drug he must have used had to be stronger than crack. His drug of choice had him looking like a wild deer that was running for his life from a gunman on the hunt. See I learned that these type of guys watch for their victims to come out of the crack house to attack. These types of attackers believe no one cares about these drug addicted prostitutes, so we can just kill them and no one will care notice. This is not true, because although we may be hooked on drugs, our families are always worried or in some type of distress. You are someone's child and believe me you are loved. This rapist placed me into a closet of that house and I thought I would never get out. I could tell that I was not his only victim. He had tools to make sure that I never got out of this closet. He nailed me in. I started to cry and scream for help once I noticed that he was gone for sure, I heard the door slam but I never heard his footsteps. Fervently, I asked the Lord to please, please allow me a chance to do better. I started turning and twisting using my shoulder to bump up against the door. I did this twice until I dint' have enough strength to open that door. There was limited space for me to move in, and once again I cried out to the Lord to please help me. Don't allow me to die like this. Once I said just that short prayer and tried to hit that door again, it flew opened. I was so much in shock of how that door just suddenly opened. I stood there for just a second and thanks to the Lord I started to run out in the street. I was on North Main Street and realized my exact location. I saw some people standing outside of their apartments. I had on just a t-shirt that I had found that somebody had thrown away since he had ripped my clothes to pieces. I was trying to find a way out of this house of hell; I will never forget this experience. When I reached those apartments where I say people standing, they laughed at me like I was a mental patient that had just escaped out of a mental institution. They didn't take me seriously when I was trying to ask each one for a phone so I could call the police. I was trying to let them know what had happened to me that I had been raped. Well this old lady that was sweeping her porch said to me come my child you need something to cover yourself with. She took me into her apartment, gave me a bathrobe and asked me what was going on with me. I told her that I had been held in that yellow house across the street all night by some man where he raped me. She said to me here is the phone, call for help my child, so I did exactly what she told me. When the officers arrived, they called for an ambulance. After making a report on what I told them, I explained to them how I was trapped in that house and rapped all night. I was transported to Richland Memorial Hospital in Columbia, SC. There I was treated very nicely by the staff. They were really concerned about what had happened to me and for my well being. Again I had to tell my story again to these people and by this time I was starting to get sick of telling it. I knew I had to tell my story in order to receive the type of help I needed in order to get catch this guy. The hospital staff would not let me go to the restroom because they needed to get a DNA sample from me to document what this man had done. The officers walked in with a plastic baggie. I'll never forget this one detective named Alvin. I remembered him so well because he stayed with me through it all. He told me how a lot of women had been raped in that area, but they never would make a statement because either they were scared of the threats that were made by the attacker or they knew the person who was doing this and was afraid to step forward. Well for me I didn't know this creep and I was damn well not afraid of anything that would happen to me. I just knew that they could get this man. I was well examined and given a good bath and some clothes to put on. The officer said he would take me where I needed to go so he could finish taking my statement. I knew this officer knew I was a street walker but he didn't treat me like one.

He treated me very well. He took me to get me something to eat and gave me hotel fare after I let him know that I was homeless. He asked me where I stayed at night. I told him wherever I can; if I didn't pick up a decent John that would take me and buy me a room for the night. Detective Alvin gave me his card and explained to me they had this man's DNA, and if I saw him to give him a call. He encouraged me to keep his cell phone number where I could remember and that was the best way I could contact him reiterating his cell phone would always been turned on. I was instructed to call him no matter what time of night it was. I went into the hotel room and I thought about all the things that this detective had talked to me about. I began thinking about the attack and how I made it out and what would happen if this man saw me again before he was caught. Looking at the time the police and the ambulance were out there, the word was out everywhere in the town. I decided I would change the area that I was hanging out in because I knew this man hadn't been captured. My attacker had told me he would kill me if I ever told anyone. I had promised him I wouldn't tell a soul if he let me live. I decided to move my business to another side of town. I had talked to a counselor that the hospital had recommended to speak with to get through this, so I did that. Detective Alvin began helping me by giving me rides back and forth to go to my counseling sessions. He decided to pay for my hotel room as long as I wanted to try to get my life in order and this went on for four months. I was now clean going to outpatient treatments thanks to this officer and my counselor which led to me landing a job. I started to work at Family Dollar on North Main Street. This detective would pick me up giving me a ride to and from work back to the hotel for my safety. I was independent now but I wasn't making enough money to get my own car. One morning I decided I would walk to work since the store was in the neighborhood not too far from where I lived. On this one particular morning, I wanted some gum and a drink to take to work. After purchasing my items, I came out of the store on my way to work. I noticed this guy standing on the side of the store. I started to walk and when I moved this guy started to move slowly behind me; the faster I walked, the faster he walked. I reached for my cell phone and I always had the detective's number on speed dial; he quickly picked up the phone. The guy was far enough behind for me to talk without him hearing me. I proceeded to tell the detective I was being followed. He told me that he was waiting for me and he came a little early this morning since he had some stops to make before taking me to work. Thank goodness he was already in the parking lot. He said for me to go straight to his car that he would be far and not to fear. He was hiding somewhere I didn't know where, but I immediately spotted his car not knowing where he was exactly. As I got into car, I locked the doors, and all of a sudden out of nowhere this guy was at the side of the car looking at me. At that very moment I started to remember all things he said to me and became so afraid. He started to punch the window when I saw the detective. He had his gun out behind him telling him to freeze police; this guy stopped in his tracks. I was so afraid now that I knew this man had been watching me and tracking me and he actually knew where I was staying. The other officers were not far behind after the detective put him in handcuffs hauling him off to jail. After the trial, this man received thirty years for rape and kidnapping. I felt much better now and felt like I could move on with my life. The detective felt like I was doing better, and I informed him I would be able to start riding the bus to and from work and to counseling. He asked me was I sure and I told him at one point you're going to have to let me fly my own wings again; so that is what he decided he would do, to let me try my wings. He said that it was nice working with me and to call him at any time that I felt I needed someone to talk to. Time went on and I continued to do well until I started to have a lot of nightmares from what had happened to me. After a year had passed, I stopped going to counseling. Now I really thought I could do good without talking to an old lady about my business. I had started to think that I was strong enough to do anything on my own now that I didn't drink or do drugs. I was feeling too confident with myself; I stopped going to Narcotics Anonymous classes. I also stopped going to alcohol classes but I continued to go to work. I started to see a lot of the old people that I used to hang out with in my work place. They would invite me to come over. I would tell my situation had changed and I was no longer drinking or drugging. In response, they would say stop on by, you don't have to drink or get high. So on one Friday night, I couldn't tell you what possessed me to go over to this old friend of mine's house. I arrived at her house around 7:30 pm, we went out to eat, caught a movie, just me and her. We laughed about some of the stupid things we used to do when we got high or was drinking. She made a statement saying let's get us a wine cooler, you can't get drunk off of that and that's what we did. We stopped at the store and got a six pack of wine coolers, and were back at my place now sipping and laughing and talking. After two of those wine coolers, we found ourselves talking about if the old people still lived around the block, wondering what they would say if they saw us. Now so we decided we would ride through the hood. When we got on the first corner, we saw an old dealer that we used to cop from. He immediately took out his bag and said here's one on me he said with pride. My friend immediately took the bait and threw it in her glove box of the car. She said oh girl we can sell this and go out tomorrow night. I said okay, well stop and let me get a Budlight, those coolers are not getting it for me. She said okay. We continued speaking and talking to old playmates from the hood; that one Budlight turned into another six pack. When we finished, that beer I couldn't remember which one of us said let's go get a pipe. Before I knew it, we were getting high and both of was speeding money like crazy. I know I was spending money I shouldn't have but I thought I could make it back up when I got paid again and I wouldn't get any more drugs. This was a lie. After a couple of days went by, I was miserable. I had spent all of my money out of my account and didn't even have money to catch the bus to go to work the next day. I managed to ask my neighbor for the money until payday so that I could make it the rest of the week. When payday finally came, it seemed like the longest of my life. My disease started to call for me. This is something I really wanted to control, but I had this thing inside me that was like a monster that's ready and can't wait to destroy my world. I can't really describe how mean this drug is, but I can share my personal insights of this to the world. Please, if you have never used this drug just continue to read this book and you will understand how real this drug really is. Take it in and listen to every word that I have to tell the world and other recovering addicts. I would like for my readers here to read and understand. I just know I can help someone to overcome this monster that is so desperate to take. It doesn't matter what race you are, it does not discriminate, so I say please look for the signs of this drug in a family or friend; you just maybe about to save a life. The next following week, at my job, my boss called me in to be drug tested and I failed. Now this is a fact that his drug does not stay in your system no more than three to five days at the most. Now that I had failed this drug test, my job was gone. I was handed my last pay check and now I went back to doing the old things that I was doing and hanging out with the same crowd again. In less than three months, I had lost my home and my power was out in my apartment. The law is you can't get government assistance if your lights are turned off in your home. So now in just a blink of an eye, I had lost it all over one night of having fun with a friend. I didn't know where I was going to stay now. I was too ashamed to call my family after all they had done for me. I didn't even know where my next meal was going to come from. The disease had taken full control over my life once again. I didn't have the desire to go out and look for another job. I needed quick fast money for bills and my habits so the only thing I could think of was prostitution, something I was really good at that was something I knew I would never forget to do. I was back on the streets and back to my old ways; my friend was back on the streets as well. We were now back to square one after all this hard work that I had put into my sobriety. I lost everything and now I was trying to get money for a hotel room again. I met this man at the truck stop at a spot I knew where I could just out run the police. I did a lot of that over the next four months. On this second time around of my addiction, this man came out of the truck stop and I asked him could I shine rims on his truck for money. I knew from the talk of guys from the past, they would tell me how good this job would pay. I used to hang with a lot of these guys so they could hook me up with the drivers so I could get money and give them a cut out of what I made just to watch my back from the police. This man that I got hooked up with had a motel room and he told me how me and him could make some money together. I would work the truck stop with the drivers and he would polish the rims. He told me we could make enough money to pay the motel bill. Every day we had money to get high and I liked the sound of that. He made things sound so easy; at first he found me a few truck drivers that would pay him for me and pay me for my services. Things were going well until one night this friend or pimp, whichever come first, wanted me to give him a freebie. He wanted free services for sex since he felt entitled to it. I went ahead and did this for him and we became very close. We started to sleep together every night that I didn't feel like going to the truck stop sometimes. I would be tired from the night before and he really didn't want to hear that. He started to fight me to the point until I would end up in the hospital. We started to fight over little stuff like food, money, water, it didn't matter; we always fought about something that was always done wrong in his eyes. If I didn't do what he wanted me to do with all these nasty old and young men, he would take me to the room and beat me. He started feeling like he should hold on to all of the money that we made together This arrangement turned sour, and was in and out of jail more times than you could count for prostituting and loitering in areas where I was not suppose to be. I would have to fight other women that would come on my turf; I had to stay clean for my clients and my clients only. I now had four counts of criminal domestic violence and was headed to the penitentiary. My friend started to do things a little different and he started to go to jail more often for being a pimp; well he was busted four times and he got six months in jail. I then felt I could get back on track and I tried. In the meantime, I met another man that became my sugar daddy. He bought me my own place. I started to straighten my life up a little. This sugar daddy had a house that he used to live in and now no one was staying there. Him and his wife were staying there but they moved on the other side of town, so now I had my own. He moved me into their old home after he moved me in. I tried my best to keep away from the people who knew me. I really didn't want to mess up my good thing that I had going on with this man. He didn't know anything about my habit, but all the girls that knew me would try to stop him and tell all of my dirty little secrets. He never would pay any attention to what they said. He felt that they were just jealous of me. This man thought he had the perfect woman or at least he thought he did. We were lying in the bed one night and we heard a voice call out from the driveway saying "Hey Mama Ru," that was the name they would call me because my son is the rapper, Lil' Ru. This voice kept calling over and over, Ma Ru calling come out and talk to me or I am not leaving.

I love you please come out and talk. I told my sugar daddy that this was the guy that I had told him about. He asked me was I going to see him again. I said no way will I ever if it means losing you, then I will never talk to him again. This man was determined to make trouble for me. I think that my sugar daddy saw in my face that I really wanted to talk to my ex after he was released from prison, he could read it in my face. Later that night my sugar daddy had to go home to his family. I knew that my ex would be back. He wasn't going to go out like that. I knew him very well and as soon as my sugar daddy's car pulled out of the driveway, my ex was coming up. I was so afraid to answer the door but he shouted out I got something for you and I knew what that was. I immediately opened the door and pretended to be glad to see him and he did the same, pretending to be happy to see me; but he knew the only reason I opened that door was because he said that he had something for me. The only light that appeared in my mind was drugs. He knew what I liked and after he made his way into the door, we instantly started to get high and have really hard sex. I knew this was dangerous and the one way to contract an unwanted STD. The number one killer of the world is having unprotected sex. I was already being tested over and over for the rape situation that I was in. I have seen a lot of females that I ran with contract HIV and die. I seen it all in these streets of hell I was one out of a million who didn't come in contact with this disease. I was blessed to have an angel somewhere flying over me. In the meantime, my sugar daddy found out about me and my ex and he really found out fast. He became so angry with me and decided he was no longer coming over to see me anymore. So I just let go and tried my best to do something to hurt him in any way that I could. He really couldn't say anything because he had to hide our relationship because he was married. Everything had to be on the down low. I came to find out that his wife was the bread winner of their family and what she said, he did.

He had written a check that his behind could not cash with me. He was riding pass the house with the girls that I running with in the street. That drug crack cocaine is so devious until you do things without thinking; crazy stuff like even. Now me and my ex decided we would make things work between us and started our thing back up at the truck stop, but this time we was going to do things a little different to where I didn't have to sleep with the truck driver. He would come and knock on the door as soon as I had the driver's clothes off. We had started to rob at anytime of the day or night. The streets were not safe at all, and the officers had started checking drivers' ID to make sure that they were a truck driver. In order to come to that truck stop you had to have ID and paperwork to prove who you were or you would go to jail for trespassing. I escaped a lot of dangerous things doing this time; that is why I feel there is someone out there that will be saved by my story. The wickedness we had going landed my friend in prison for a year and I received a two year sentence for conspiracy to strong arm robbery, but I got out in six months on good behavior. They never could really prove that I was the woman with him. He never said that I was with him. When I got out of jail, I went to see did I still have that house, and I found out that the old man that lived across the street was making sure that everything was kept put up for me. The neighbor knew my sugar daddy and the trouble I had gotten into with my ex. He never liked him, my friend, why, I couldn't answer that question but I know that my neighbor cared what happened to me once I was released. My sugar daddy started to speak to me again. I assumed my neighbor had explained to him about me and my situation. When I got off the bus I went to my neighbor he told me everything was okay that my sugar daddy wanted me to call him. I hurried and ran to the phone booth and called him. He picked up on the first ring; told me that he had just come off a cruise with his wife. Once he got to the house, we quickly started to make up for lost time. He handed me a one hundred dollar bill and now I just knew I was back in business with this man. I decided this time that I would not smoke the crack but I would sell the stuff. Wow what a huge mistake that was. It started off good but my house was there on the main road. Once the word was out, it took off really well. Money was flowing like milk and honey. I had every prostitute there and all the other dealers wanted a piece of the action. I had made a special room for anyone who brought a man over and needed a place to do business. All they had to do was knock and pay and I was game for it. After my friend served his time, he appeared one day out of the blue at my door step. I welcomed him in since my sugar daddy was not coming over that much. He e knew what I had going on and he didn't want any part in it. He let a lot of things go on the way I wanted to go. To keep peace between me and him and his wife whom he never wanted to find out, my friend decided he would not cause any problems for me. He wanted to help me out and that's what he did. He was really a big help because people respected him. I started to fall back in love with my ex and that's when all hell broke loose. I started using with him and after a long night of hot sex and drinking. It led me back down that dark road again; to me this man and drug was my God. I worshipped them both. Every time I went back to this drug, things seemed to get worst but at the time, I didn't see it coming. It took me all the way to the bottom, my ex pretended to love me but the habit had him to where if I didn't give him when he wanted it; he started having me to rob his friends pretending not to know anything about it. I found out later that it was him through the words in the street that I was not giving him what he wanted that he would find a way to get it and he did. I was robbed four times within two months time and that was it for me. All the money was gone on that last robbery, so I decided I would walk the street. I thought that would be safer than a gun being thrown in my face every week or every other week. Things really got bad for me, and this time I was raped again over and over. I cut and stabbed so many people until I lost count of the Johns; I didn't know if they lived or died. After I was done with them, I became cold hearted toward everyone. I started to get in the cars with any John and not giving him time to rape me if that was his intentions. I would pull a knife or gun and just get what I needed and make serious threats to kill. I got what I wanted by any means necessary. I really wanted what I wanted and I didn't care who lived or who died. It was all about me. I had this part of town so afraid they were beginning to get scared to pick up any woman. I was getting in cars with guys and looking so humble and peaceful until they mentioned to me about the woman slasher not knowing they were in the car with her. It seemed I would never get my life back together after this. I tried calling my family but the attempts were all I could do. I never made it to talk to anyone in my family. My brother-in-law happened to see me at the Exxon Station on Fairfield Road, he recognized me and how I don't know but he did. He called me over and I went to see what he wanted. He told me I was going to die. He told me that he would send the rest of the family for me and that's what happened. I was rescued by my family and sent to rehab. I was in and out now. I was thinking clearly but still didn't have the right mind set to do right. Something really had a hold of me. I went back into this world after being released from rehab. I was addicted when I was out in the streets, and my body was worn out. I had been up for two days. I got with this man and gave him the benefit of the doubt. I didn't do any harm to this man and we went to the ATM machine. He drew out two hundred dollars and we went to my place. He liked it, saying my place was nice, cozy, and quaint. I called a dealer I knew to come and sell us some drugs. It didn't take very long for the word to get out. That truck driver was at my house and my friend was at my door asking me was it okay to come in; I didn't trust him at all. After what he had done to me so I kept a close eye on him. He seemed to be in a calm mood, and he apologized because he knew how I felt about what he had done to me. I stayed ready like a lion ready to get his prey after a long winter with no food. We laughed, played cards; we enjoyed ourselves at least that's what we thought. We was doing that sick mind always make you thing you are having a good time. This went on for two days of no sleep, just us sitting there talking and having what you would call a crack part. This driver was spending all of his money and when the money started to get low, my friend knew this and my friend he knew this. He started to call the man off to the side and tell us where he could get a better deal for the money he was spending. The driver started to go along with what he said since his mind was like a child now. He could not make his own decisions and my ex friend knew how to play games with a person who was not an everyday crack smoker. We were now down with the cigarettes and beer so we decided to go out and get some. We sent my friend to go get the drugs while me and the truck driver went to the store. When we arrived at the house, sure enough he had kept his word and was there with the package, but one thing about this package was the size of it. We didn't get what our money had paid for. At first, I didn't say anything. I played along with this and we started to drink all of a sudden. He said let's gamble, we said okay. Now I am wondering where in the hell did he get money from. I still sat there with no response knowing that he had pulled one of his games again. We kept on playing cards and he had won all of the money so he wasn't worried about what he had lost in the card game. The truck driver said let's go back to the ATM. Now the driver was feeling pretty good and we all were. I called my friend off to the side and said baby let me get my cut out of all of this. He quickly got mad and started to yell at me as loudly as he could. He was yelling so loudly that the truck driver could hear what was going on. My friend said he wasn't gonna give me shit and told the truck driver to get his own bitch. I told him to get the hell out of my house; the party was over for him. He went back into the living room and asked the driver to give him a ride across town where the real women were. After he done cleaned me out, I was now in a rage. He kept saying things like I wasn't even in the room and I was nothing but a truck hopping whore. The driver said man don't worry, she's cool, she been cool with me every since I been here, she been good to me so let's just go get some more money and finish having a good time. Well that's not what he wanted to do. He wanted to go and party with some other people. I told him right in front of the truck driver that he done robbed us and now he's ready to leave. I knew I couldn't trust this man. He decided to get bold and slapped me. He slapped me to the floor to the point of darkness. I had never been hit that hard that I could recall in my life, not even in the streets fighting. I knew this man was very abusive and when he couldn't get things to go his way what he would do to me in the past. I should have never let him in the door. Some people were walking by that knew me and stopped in. The argument was so heated they would go ahead on by their business. He pulled his hand up to slap me again and I was not going for it a second time. I reached over my fireplace and got my knife and stabbed him. The knife hit my friend that was trying to break us up in the chest. Things happened so fast that it was scary. I dropped the knife after I saw what had happened to my friend. I really didn't mean to stab my friend so I ran to a neighbor's house and told them what had happened and they told me to have a seat until they went to see what was going on. My neighbor came back to his house where I was waiting for him to return and tell me the news. He told me that they were sitting there partying and he told him that it was an accident that I didn't mean to do that to him. We had been up for days and he thought I was out of my mind, so I went back to my house. By the time I got myself together to go back they had invited a girl into my house just that fast. I knew this girl and I knew that she was a street walker. I used to walk the street with this lady. She had the crack pipe in her mouth when I walked in the door. The music was jumping as if nothing had just happened. My friend that was trying to stop the fight had put a maxi pad over the stab wound with a rope tied around his back to the front to hold it in place to try to stop the bleeding. This was so disgusting to me but I was in such a rage about the woman being in my house now until I went straight to her and began to fight her. We tore everything up in the house, ant the truck driver broke the fight up. Me and him left to go up the street so I could cool off and talk. He remembered that we had given my friend some money and he wanted to go back and get it. He let me out of the car up the street and said he would be right back; well right back never came. I ran into my cousin from my hometown of where I grew up in Ridgeway, SC. He said he was coming from the club and asked me what was wrong with me. I told him all the details of what happened and he got me into the car. He told me now to never leave my own home for nobody, so I took his advice and he let me out in the front of my door of my home. I went in and went straight to my bedroom; the sleep was coming down on me now after all these nights of staying up. I went into the bedroom and as soon as I laid my head on the pillow, I was asleep. The next morning I heard a knock on the door and it was my cousin that had given me the ride from the night before. He was checking to see if I was okay, at least that's what I thought it was, but boy was I wrong. He was coming to tell me that my brother had died this morning or something yesterday. He was not sure but his mother had called him and told me the news. I started to cry and that's something that I never did. The streets had me tough and to cry was a sign of weakness. I really didn't think I had any feelings until I got this news about my brother;

he asked me how my friend was doing that got stabbed last night. I told him he was in the room trying to get some sleep since we all had been up for days. My cousin asked me was I going to need a ride to the country. I told him to tell the family that I got the news and I would be up there later. I immediately went to the phone booth and called my older sister collect. I knew she would be the only one that would accept my call even if I was in jail she would always accept my calls. She was more like the mother of the family and told me to be in one place because she would send someone to get me. She told me to stay put because nobody was going to run all over Columbia looking for me. My sister sent my brother's girlfriend to pick me up; I think they worked together and she asked her to pick me up the following day. My friend that I was in the argument with said that he didn't want to go so I quickly said okay because he looked a mess anyway. I really didn't want my family to see me with him. I was already looking bad enough, and they really didn't need to see what I was hanging around a crack addicted person. I had managed to find something to wear to the funeral. The drugs had me to where I didn't have anything but hand me downs, I didn't have to live like this. It was all my choice. I had family that really loved me and wanted me out of the street. A lot of my family had washed their hands with me because of the bad choices I was making in life. I knew my lifestyle was not pleasing to my family. I felt like they were very ashamed of me so I just stayed out of their way and out sight. I found out later on that one of my sisters was not crying because of the death of our brother, but she took a look at me in the church at the funeral and started to cry about me. When all this was over and I returned back to Columbia, I walked into the door of the house. All was very quiet so I started to call my friend's name out over and over again but he never responded. I walked into the guest bedroom and there was my friend that I had stabbed nights before lying on his back dead. I shook him and called his name. He never answered or moved. He had on a t-shirt where I could see through it. I felt his face and it was cold as ice. I knew he had been dead for a while and I looked again and the t-shirt was stuck to him. I pulled it up and he had a piece of duck tape over the wound. His wound must have become infected while I was gone. He had assured me that he would go to the doctor by the time I returned from my brother's funeral. This was the worst thing that I have ever seen in all my days. I found a sheet and covered him up and ran as fast as I could to get help. No one seemed to believe me so I called the police. I didn't tell them who I was but I made the call and got them over to where the body was. I was so afraid at this point until all I could do was turn to drugs. I got me a John and he helped me to get what I needed. I went into the woods and looked while they brought my friend's body out my house. I was crying uncontrollably and the drug started to make me bold. I came out of the woods and asked the police why were they around my house. I knew good and well what I had done. The man that had the strips must have been the sergeant and he asked me did I know who lived here. I said of course, I do. He stated to me that they had gotten a phone call saying there was a dead body in this house and he was just following up the call. He asked me did I know anything about that. I said no real fast. He asked me could he take a look around. I said its okay by me, help yourself. He asked when was the last time I been home, I told him four to five days ago that I was out of town because of my brother's death. I showed him the obituary to clear myself o f what was going on. He told me to stand outside that he had to call in some more help to try to find out what happened here in my home. I pretended not to know anything so I started to cry. I acted so surprised at what I was just told by the police officers. See when you are on this type of drug you have no control over your actions or wonder why it is necessary to tell a lie for no reason. The police officers stayed there for about thirty minutes or better. They called the coroner and after they carried him away, I was told by the officer not to go anywhere because another detective was on the way to question me. This detective looked very suspicious of me, so I told him that I would be over to the neighbor's house if they needed me and my neighbor sat there and we were both so sad about what had happened. My neighbor was an old white man that was always there for people like us that didn't have family to talk to or if you were hungry he would give you something to eat. He started to tell me how my friend had come over and told him that the stabbing was an accident and I was in such a rage that night with no sleep. The detectives started calling me across the street, and when I got across the street, the officer started to question me immediately. The first thing they asked me was did I know what had happened to his chest. I replied maybe something happened before he came here to stay. I told him no sir I don't know what happened to his chest so the officer gave me a card and told me to call him if I found out anything. I said okay and went into the house to pack me some clothes and left to go stay in the nearest crack house I knew. I knew they would let me stay as long as I had money to cop drugs so I put the few rags that I had in the crack house and went out to make me some money to leave town. Before I could leave town, within the next few hours I was stopped while walking the strip and taken to the police station for more questioning. I stayed there all night until the next morning. I was charged with murder and I was transported to the Alvin S. Glenn Detention Center. The only thing I could conclude to why I was charged was because they found someone that knew what had happened and a statement had been made. I stayed in jail for four months before they even assigned me a public defender. I was called one day by this white guy and I thought there was going to more questions but this was not the case. He was my attorney and he called me into this private room and told me who he was. He told me I had to be completely honest with him in order for him to help me. He felt that I didn't stand a chance with the evidence that he had against me, so I immediately called my oldest sister and told her what this public defender had said. She told me that she would talk with the rest of the family to see if she could get me a real lawyer to help because they felt that it was not my fault. My family started to be supportive of me. I promised my family that I would not let them down if they just helped me through this. I knew I had lied to my family so many times until they just didn't have any belief in me anymore. I really started to thank God when whatever my oldest sister said to the rest of the family, it worked and I started to receive money and letters from my other sisters, cousins, and nieces. I was so pleased to see all the support I received. I was really pleased and at this time I called upon the name of Jesus and promised myself and God to never to go back to that life. I went to God with all my heart and I've been living for him every since. When I saw my lawyer again, it was a paid lawyer and he was ready to fight for my freedom. He told me he was going to get my motion of discovery and that would tell me every person that said something for me or against me. He told me by the statement of my neighbor and the victim's father that I stood a good chance in court. After two years of being in jail, I was sent to trial. My charges were downgraded from murder to manslaughter and that was really good news. I found out when I got to the courtroom I had my neighbor there and the victim's father testifying that he didn't want me to get one day in prison. This was all of the plans that God had for me. I was sentenced to ten years in prison and I only did seven with my good behavior. My time was cut even shorter. While being in prison, I saw a lot of things. Death came to my feet one morning when I was not looking for an inmate who was killed at my feet. This was the wildest things I had ever seen. You see things like this on television but you never think you would see it for real but I did. I called and told my family over and over that from what I had seen, they would never have to worry about me turning back around. I just thank Gold to still be alive in a place like this. I was in a place with people that were never going to see the light of day again outside of prison. Food is not a bowl of cherries and I often found bugs in my food. I almost had a heart attack from what they put in the food. I was rushed to the see the doctor several times and was told that I could not eat that food in there because of the starch. My family had to really send me a lot of money because what I could eat I could buy from the prison store. This food was really expensive and after coming home, we added up the money that my family had spent which equaled a small fortune. I wouldn't wish what happened to me on my worst enemy. I knew with all the mistakes I had made in my life, I had someone else sacrificing for me. My family came to see me faithfully; every weekend I had a visit. I had a sister that lived in Charlotte, NC that came to see me and believed in me more than I believed in myself. I made her a promise after she had dealt with my mess for twenty five years; I knew I had to make a change not just for my family but for myself. I started going to bible school to learn more about the Lord and what he can do for me. I knew there was no way I could do this alone. I used the penitentiary to my advantage. I used all the tools they gave me and I worked to become a better person in life. When I walked out those doors after my time was up in the penitentiary, I was now ready for home. I was not sure where I was going to go but my family had it all planned out for me. I was going to live with my niece in Greenville, SC and when I was released, the next day they had a big glorious party for me that I will never forget. The things my family did kept me strong and it's the love of my family that keeps me going every day. I am saying this to say that if you have a family member that is going through what you are reading now, please help them no matter how many times they may have failed. They can change and with a support group from their family, that person could never fail. I know because I've been clean for fourteen years and still going strong so please don't just read my book, understand the meaning that I am trying to get out t o the world. I wanted to go back to work but my record was not clean. This story I am telling is for real. I got a job; everywhere I went to apply my record never showed up on a background check so don't be afraid to move forward. Let God guide your footsteps. I went to college and I now have my associate's in massage therapy and medical assisting so it can be done. I have now met this most wonderful man that God could possibly give any women on this earth. I met him just coming home to visit the family and ran into him getting gas. We used to be old lovers from the past. I guess he thought I was still the same way until he walked over and talked to me and we decide we would go out for dinner. Within two years we were married and we are still together. God blessed us with two beautiful twins at this time since he had previously lost his wife, and God brought him to me and I can't ask God for more.